THE NATURE KIDS GUIDE TO

KOMODO DRAGONS

DAVID ANDERSON

LP Media Inc. Publishing
Text copyright © 2026 by LP Media Inc.
All rights reserved.

For information address LP Media Inc. Publishing,
30012 Variolite St NW, Princeton MN 55371
www.lpmedia.org

Publication Data

Komodo Dragons
The Nature Kid's Guide to Komodo Dragons — First edition.

Summary: "Learn all about Komodo Dragons, the Nature Kid Way"
— Provided by publisher.

ISBN: 979-8-89818-123-9

[1. Komodo Dragons – Non-Fiction] I. Title.

Title: The Nature Kid's Guide to Komodo Dragons

CONTENTS

HOT AND HARSH

Komodo dragons dig burrows in the ground. These underground shelters help them stay cool during the hottest parts of the day and keep them warm at night.

Hiss! A Komodo dragon flicks its tongue in the heat.

Komodo dragons live in hot, dry places. These giant lizards can live in several types of habitats.

They roam through tropical forests with tall trees. They walk across dry grasslands with brown grass. They rest in rocky valleys under the hot sun.

The weather can be harsh. It often gets hotter than 95 degrees! Rain falls for only a few months each year. The rest of the time, the land stays dry.

But Komodo dragons are built for this tough life. Their bodies handle heat well.

ISLAND LIFE

Thump! A Komodo dragon walks across a sandy beach.

Komodo dragons live only in Indonesia. There are only five islands in the world where they can be found.

The largest is Komodo Island. These islands are hot and dry for most of the year.

Komodo National Park protects most of these dragons. Rangers watch over them. Visitors come from around the world to see these amazing creatures in the wild.

The island of Komodo is only about 22 miles long. That is smaller than most big cities.

MEGA MONSTERS

Stomp! A huge Komodo dragon moves through the grass.

Komodo dragons are the largest lizards on Earth. They can grow up to 10 feet long. That is longer than most cars!

Males are bigger than females. A large male can weigh over 150 pounds. Some reach 200 pounds or more.

Their size helps them hunt big animals. They can take down deer and wild pigs. Even water buffalo are not safe from these mighty hunters.

A Komodo dragon's tail is as long as its body. The tail helps with balance.

DEADLY DESIGN

Snap! A young Komodo dragon sneeks up on it's prey.

Komodo dragons have bodies made for hunting. Their skulls are long and flat, and strong neck muscles help them pull and tear meat.

Their teeth are small, but are sharp and curved. Each tooth has jagged edges like a saw. These edges can slice through tough skin and meat.

Komodo dragons also have sharp claws. Each foot has five toes with long claws. They use these claws to grip prey and dig burrows.

Their strong tails help with hunting too. A tail whip can knock down other animals.

TONGUE
TRICKS
12

Swoosh! A Komodo dragon waves its tongue in the air.

Komodo dragons smell with their tongues. They flick their tongues in and out. The tongue picks up tiny bits from the air.

The tongue is long and forked. The two tips each catch different smells.

The dragon brings its tongue inside its mouth. A special organ reads the smells. This tells the dragon which direction to go to find food.

Komodo dragons can smell dead animals from over two miles away.

13

TOUGH SCALES

Scrape! A Komodo dragon rubs against a rough rock.

Komodo dragons have tough skin. Their scales have tiny bones inside. These bones are called **osteoderms**.

The bony scales work like armor. They stop bites. They stop scratches. Other Komodo dragons cannot hurt them easily.

Young dragons do not have these bones yet. The armor grows as they get older. It takes about four years for the bony scales to fully form.

Scientists only discovered Komodo dragon osteoderms in 2019 using special scans.

BIG BITES

Chomp! A Komodo dragon bites into a meal. This lizard is hungry.

Komodo dragons only eat meat. They hunt deer, pigs, and water buffalo. They also eat smaller animals like birds and snakes.

These lizards can eat a lot at once. A dragon can eat up to 80 percent of its own body weight in one meal.

Komodo dragons swallow large chunks of food. They do not chew much. Instead, their strong stomach acid breaks down bones. They do spit out fur though.

Komodo dragons also eat carrion, or animals that are already dead.

AMBUSH ATTACK
FUN FACT!
Komodo dragons sometimes knock down large prey with their strong, powerful tails.
18

Crunch! A Komodo dragon hides near some bushes. It waits for prey to walk by.

Komodo dragons are ambush hunters. They do not chase prey for long distances. Instead, they wait and hide.

A dragon picks a spot near a trail. Deer and pigs walk by on these paths. The dragon stays very still. It can wait for hours.

When an animal comes close, the dragon attacks fast. It rushes out and bites hard. The bite has **venom** that weakens the prey. The dragon then follows the hurt animal until it falls down.

TOP DOG

Growl! A Komodo dragon stands tall. It rules this island.

Komodo dragons are **apex predators**. This means they are at the top of the food chain. Adult Komodo dragons have no enemies. But young dragons are hunted by other animals.

These dragons are the largest lizards in the world. Their big size helps them catch large prey. No animals are safe from a hungry dragon.

No other predator on these islands can compete. Komodo dragons are the top dog of their islands.

Komodo dragons store fat in their tails. This helps them survive for over a month without eating or drinking.

FIGHT BACK

Snarl! A Komodo dragon hisses at a threat. It is ready to fight.

Adult Komodo dragons have few natural enemies. But sometimes they must defend themselves from other dragons.

When scared, a dragon puffs up its throat. This makes it look bigger. It also hisses loudly to warn enemies away.

A dragon can use its sharp claws to scratch. Its strong tail can whip and hit hard.

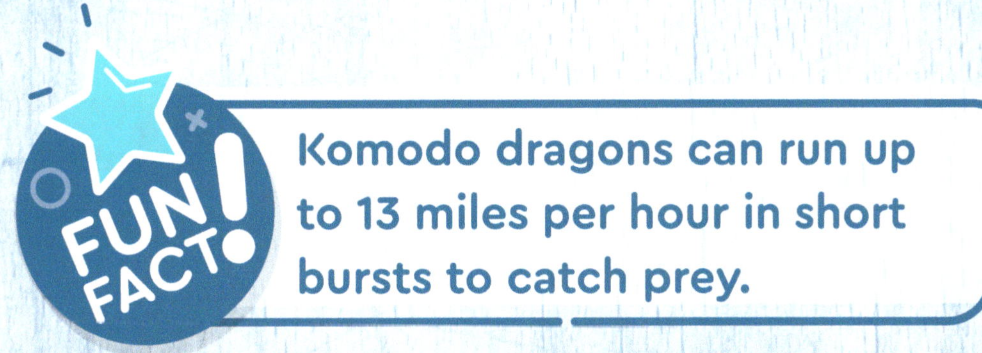

SWIFT SWIMMERS

Splash! A Komodo dragon dives into the sea. It swims toward an island.

Komodo dragons are good swimmers. They can swim between islands.

These big lizards paddle with their legs. Their long tails push them through the water. This helps them hold their heads above the surface.

Komodo dragons swim to find food on other islands. Some swim more than a kilometer to reach new shores.

Komodo dragons can swim for hours. Thats how they travel between their island homes.

SUN SEEKERS

Rustle! A Komodo dragon lies on warm rocks. It soaks up the sun.

Komodo dragons are cold-blooded. They cannot make their own body heat. They need the sun to warm up.

In the morning, dragons bask on rocks or open ground. The sun heats their bodies. This gives them energy to move and hunt.

When it gets too hot, they rest in the shade. They also dig burrows to stay cool at night.

Komodo dragons have a special gland near their eyes. It removes extra salt after they swim in the ocean.

LONE LIZARDS

Male Komodo dragons may fight each other if they meet in the same territory.

A Komodo dragon walks alone. It does not need a group.

Komodo dragons live alone. They do not have families. They do not form packs.

Each dragon has its own space. It walks alone through the tall grass. It looks for food by itself. It finds a cool place to rest.

Most dragons stay in the same area their whole lives. They know every trail. They know every hiding spot.

Dragons meet to eat big prey. They also meet to find a mate. Then they go back to living alone.

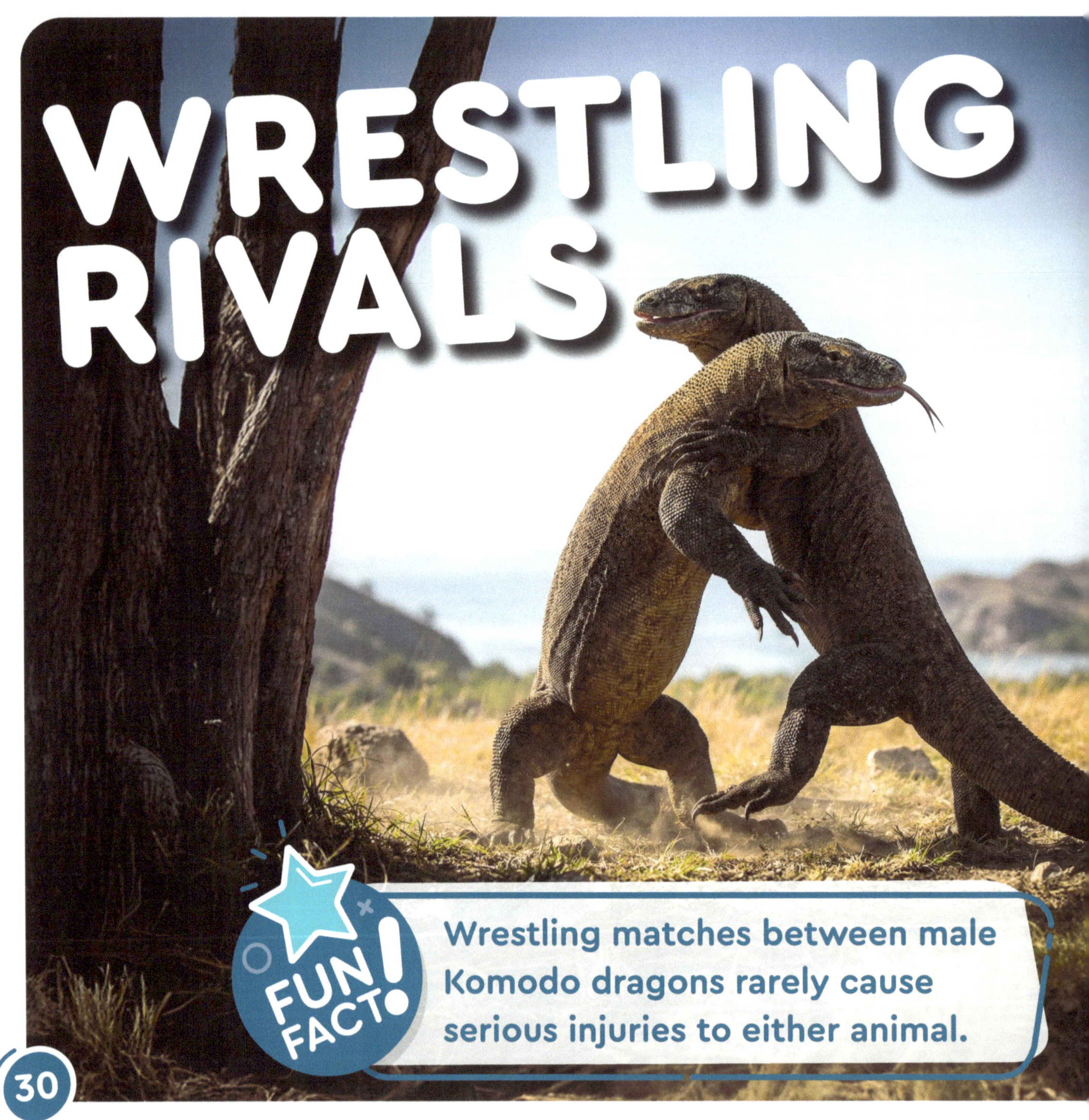

WRESTLING RIVALS
FUN FACT!
Wrestling matches between male Komodo dragons rarely cause serious injuries to either animal.
30

Rumble! Two male Komodo dragons push each other hard.

Male Komodo dragons fight to win a mate. They stand on their back legs and wrestle. They push and grab with their front legs. Their long tails help them balance.

The dragons try to knock each other down. They bite and scratch with sharp claws. These fights can last for many minutes.

Sometimes both dragons get hurt. Blood drips from their cuts. But their tough armor protects them from serious harm.

The winner gets to mate. The loser walks away to live alone again.

TINY
HATCHLINGS

Crack! A baby Komodo dragon breaks out of its egg.

Female Komodo dragons lay about 20 eggs at a time. The eggs stay buried in the ground for 7 to 8 months.

Baby dragons are called **hatchlings**. They are about 40 centimeters long when they hatch. That makes them smaller than a house cat.

Hatchlings climb trees right away and live there for their first few years. This keeps them safe from bigger dragons that might eat them.

Hatchlings have bright yellow and green bands on their skin. These colors fade as they grow into adults.

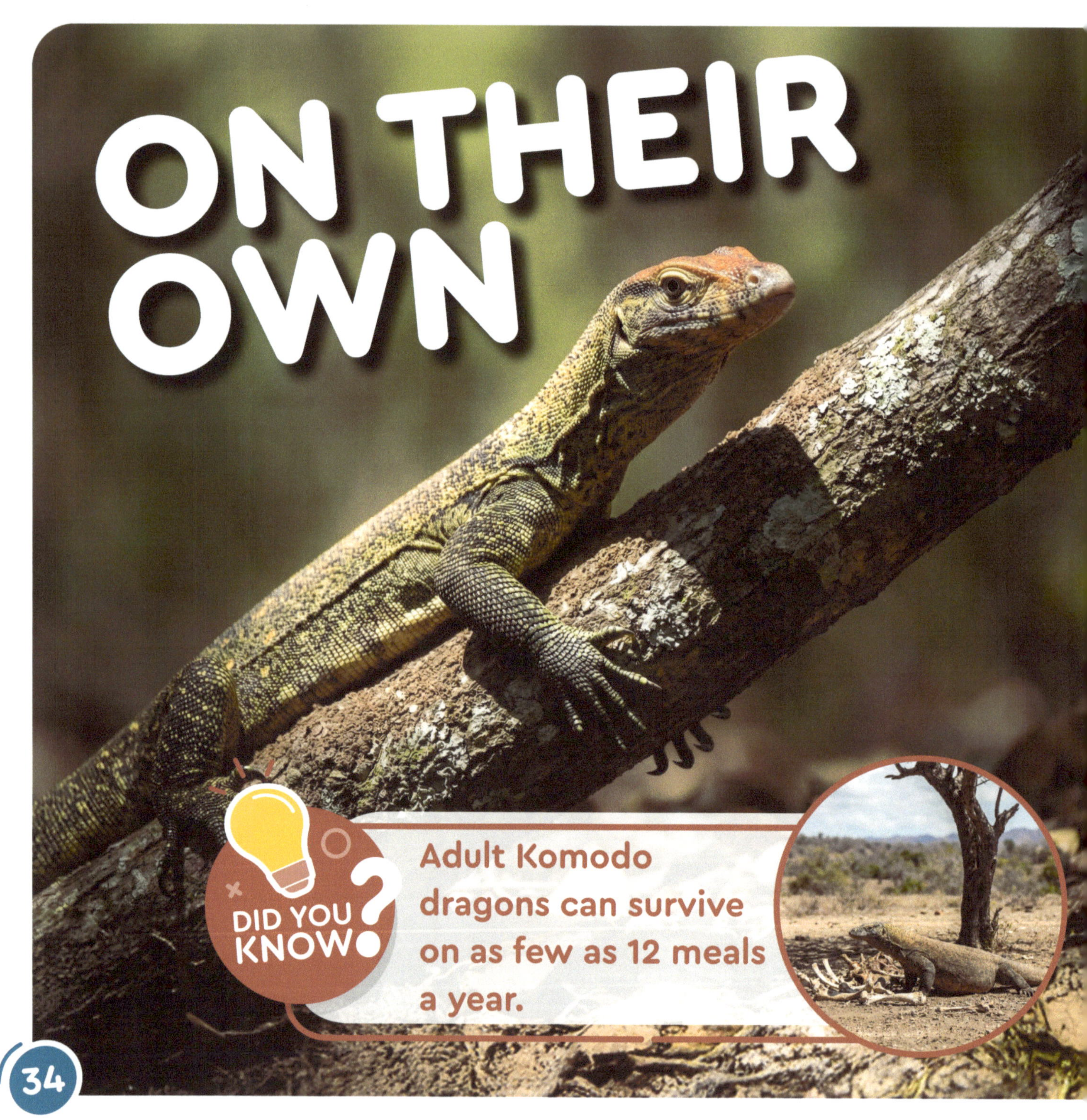

ON THEIR
OWN

DID YOU KNOW?

Adult Komodo dragons can survive on as few as 12 meals a year.

Screech! A young Komodo dragon sits in a tree alone.

Baby Komodo dragons do not get help from their parents. The mother guards her nest for about three months, but then she leaves and does not come back.

Hatchlings must find their own food right away. This means hunting insects, small lizards, and bird eggs all by themselves.

Young dragons stay in trees for up to four years. When they get big enough, they move to the ground. By then, they know how to survive on their own.

SHRINKING SPACE

Roar! A Komodo dragon looks for food. Its home is getting smaller.

Komodo dragons are endangered. Their numbers are shrinking every year.

People cut down forests to build farms and homes. This destroys the places where dragons live and hunt.

When forests disappear, deer and wild pigs leave too. These animals are the dragon's main food. Hungry dragons cannot survive.

Some islands have lost all their dragons. On Padar Island, no dragons have been seen since 1975. Scientists work hard to stop this from happening on other islands.

HELPING HANDS

Grunt! A ranger checks on a Komodo dragon. She wants to make sure they are healthy.

People work hard to save Komodo dragons. Komodo National Park keeps most of them safe. Rangers guard the dragons. They protect their homes too.

Scientists study the dragons. They count how many live on each island. This helps them know if dragons are doing well.

Other groups help too. They plant trees. They teach people how to live near dragons safely.

Tourists come to see the dragons. This gives the park money to help save them.

GLOSSARY

osteoderms

Tiny bones inside an animal's skin that work like armor.

apex predators

Animals at the very top of the food chain with no enemies that hunt them.

carrion

Dead animals that other animals find and eat.

venom

A poison that some animals make in their bodies to hurt other animals.

hatchlings

Baby animals that have just come out of their eggs.